Doing The Work To Become A Better You!

30 days of Inspiration to help you along the way.

By Dr. Toi Dennis

Table of Contents

Dedication

To My Beautiful Daughter Genesis....

My life, my joy, my world. You are the greatest blessing that I could have ever received. You are the reason why I have worked so hard to be a better woman and a better mother. You brighten my day! You are smart, you are kind and you are beautiful.

We have experienced a lot just the two of us; however, no matter what life has brought us your sweet spirit has remained the same. Thank you for being so mature, understanding the sacrifices that it has taken to reach all the monumental milestones in my life thus far. I do it all for you! Always remember that my prayer for you is to supercede any of the accomplishments I have ever made. With God on your side, you can do anything. The favor of God is all over your life. I love you forever! You're my greatest inspiration.

Love Always, Mommie

Acknowledgments

I would like to thank each and everyone that has supported me in my journey. Your prayers and support have been amazing. Special Thank You to Dr. Jackie Knight for pushing me through this journey and keeping me accountable through the process. May this book bless each of your lives, as it has blessed mines dearly. Feeling both honoured and privileged to share the things that have been placed on my heart. I know that God has given me insight to share with the world to help impact and change lives daily. His grace and mercy is always sufficient.

Dr. Toi

Doing The Work To Become A Better You!

30 days of Inspiration to help you along the way.

Preface

The beginning of a new season is the perfect time to renew your perspective and look at life with a fresh and positive outlook. Daily we are faced with all types of challenges that life may bring but through prayer and an encouraging word we can make it through the day. I can remember sitting in the living room in silence one-night thinking about the past, the challenges I've had to face and how it has taken a lot of work to get to where I am today. Some days were harder than others but I found myself often not making progress because I wasn't doing the work. Working on ourselves to become a better person so that we can live out our purpose and be who God has called us to be is important. In order to become a better person, you must do the work. Whatever it is that you must work on to become a better person I want you to know that it's possible.

Sometimes we just need to be reminded of how far God has brought us and the promises that he has for our lives. Journaling allows you to vent out your feelings, organize your thoughts, track your progress and find yourself all at once. Sure, you can go to therapy, go on a mindful walk or allow time to take the lead to find yourself, but all of those aren't seen by the naked eye. When you journal, you allow yourself to see your progress and most importantly find yourself. You are what you think, let your thoughts Inspire you.

Now that you have chosen to do THE WORK for the next 30 days, I want to encourage and inspire you as you embark on this journey. I will be standing in faith with you asking God to help your stay committed. It's my prayer that you will see transformation in your life as a result of your desire to live an intentional life in Him.

I pray this book will help you get a picture of the purpose God has for you and allow you to see your future from His perspective.

Let's Get Started!

For I know the plans I have for you," says the Lord. "They are plans for good and not for disaster, to give you a future and a hope. Jeremiah 29:11 nlt

DAY 1
You Are Not Alone

First of all, let me say how excited I am about your decision to Inspire with me for the next 30 days and DO THE WORK. I believe that you will experience hope in Christ and see changes in your life daily as you purse this godly goal and take daily action toward your commitment.

You can do this! One reason I know you can because you are not alone. There will be days where you may not feel like making the effort to do THE WORK. Just remember, you are creating a new habit in your life. Each day you take the required actions, you are one step closer to making an intentional difference in your life and your future.

"Success at anything isn't by accident, but by decision".

Be Blessed! Be Inspired!

NOTES

_____

_____

_____

_____

_____

_____

_____

_____

_____

_____

_____

_____

_____

_____

_____

_____

DAY 2

No Worries

One thing that separates those from how to succeed from those who fail is a decision not to give in to the fear or failure. What you think about is important. If you spend your time concerned about not always getting things right, then most likely you won't.

In the bible Apostle Paul gives four specific action steps to take daily with the promise that peace will follow.

1. Pray Daily.

2. Ask humbly.

3. Give thanksgiving daily.

4. Tell yourself the truth.

"One the greatest gifts we can give ourselves is to be sure our thinking matches what we believe, and then start behaving in line with those truths".

Be Blessed! Be Inspired!

NOTES

_____

_____

_____

_____

_____

_____

_____

_____

_____

_____

_____

_____

_____

_____

_____

_____

_____

_____

_____

DAY 3

Choose Freedom and Peace

Now that you have started to do the work, you're well on your way to reinventing the life by focusing on yourself, but sometimes this type of life change involves identifying an underlying problem. This is where you need to think through and discover the root of the problem and the real issues you face, not just symptoms.

Prayer is a great place to start! Ask God to reveal the truth to you so you can address the real problem and issue, then make huge strides towards achieving your goal over the next 30 days.

"Freedom and Peace happen at the intersection of God's intentional love for you, the gifts and talents he has given you and your willingness to be obedient and take action is the key."

Be Blessed! Be Inspired!

NOTES

_____

_____

_____

_____

_____

_____

_____

_____

_____

_____

_____

_____

_____

_____

_____

DAY 4

Let love Break Down Prison Walls

What are something's you fear? What keeps you imprisoned inside walls of fear emotionally? Fear can do strange things to people. It brings out behaviours that wouldn't be typical under different circumstances.

- Fear destroys relationships

- Fear steals your motivation

- Fear can lead to bad decisions

- Fear causes distrust

You can't afford to throw in the towel because of your fears!

"Freedom from fear is the result when you embrace the truth of God's love."

Be Blessed! Be Inspired!

NOTES

_____

_____

_____

_____

_____

_____

_____

_____

_____

_____

_____

_____

_____

_____

_____

_____

_____

_____

DAY 5

It's Really Worth It

Have you been tempted to give up on doing THE WORK this week? I only ask the question because sometimes it's easier to stop pressing forward and just throw in the towel and not purse what God has for you. Wherever you find yourself today in your commitment, know that doing THE WORK for 30 days and beyond is worth it. Each action you take will catapult you right into the success God has for you.

"There is a line that represents a point where you have to make a decision, and then take action."

Be Blessed! Be Inspired!

NOTES

_____

_____

_____

_____

_____

_____

_____

_____

_____

_____

_____

_____

_____

_____

_____

_____

DAY 6

Words of Encouragement

The words you speak matter. They can have the authority to empower or destroy, your life and lives of those you speak with. Encouraging words bring life and hope to the hearer. As you continue doing THE WORK, share your goal with a few close friends you trust and then ask them to help you by offering encouragement. If they know you very well, they'll give you words you need at just the right time, like I hope I'm doing as you continue to read this book.

You can take it a step further and focus on speaking words of encouragement to those friends you've shared THE WORK with.

"The words you speak change lives."

Be Blessed! Be Inspired!

NOTES

_____

_____

_____

_____

_____

_____

_____

_____

_____

_____

_____

_____

_____

_____

_____

_____

_____

DAY 7

Peace for Parents

You've made it to the seventh day of your 30-day challenge CONGRATULATIONS! Today I want to share a word of encouragement to those who took the challenge to be more intentional parents.

How many times has your overbearing hand of discipline provoked an already rebellious child to lash out even more against you? Or perhaps your laid-back attitude allowed your child an opportunity to dismiss your direction? The answer is to find a balance of discipline, the fine line that varies according to each child. The balance of discipline is not a simple task for any parent, but especially the parent who wrestles with over-or under compensating for the guilt or self-doubt they're experiencing in their role as a parent.

"Let the Word of God come alive for your situation, and experience the hope of God's help to parent His child and yours."

Be Blessed! Be Inspired!

NOTES

_____

_____

_____

_____

_____

_____

_____

_____

_____

_____

_____

_____

_____

_____

_____

_____

DAY 8
Give God The Glory!

As you start your eighth day of doing THE WORK, remember to keep your focus on pleasing Christ. If you've missed something's here or there in your commitment, don't let that give you a reason to quit. Stay committed and stay connected to God.

Sometimes we fail to seek God when things are going well, then when the bottom seems to fall out of our lives, we turn to Him. Don't wait until the bottom falls out, but be intentional and seek God now.

Each moment spent with God prepares you for what lies ahead. When you face adversity, you can remain confident in your faith in Christ because you've been taken the time to build those spiritual muscles. You can remain strong through the challenges' life brings. Stay intentional and give God the Glory!

"Living intentionally means doing THE WORK each day and leads to an abundant life in Christ. "

Be Blessed! Be Inspired!

NOTES

_____

_____

_____

_____

_____

_____

_____

_____

_____

_____

_____

_____

_____

_____

_____

_____

_____

_____

DAY 9

Don't Let It Stress You Out

I truly believe that living an intentional life in Christ is the only way you can accomplish those things you believe matter most. We all have good intentions, whether it's to be a good parent or partner, to excel on the job, or to be successful in general. But often what happens when things don't go exactly as intended, you begin to stress out.

You're already ahead of the game on this because you've made a commitment. You've focused on doing THE WORK with a purpose of making it work. When you allow external situations to drive your life and you're not intentionally committed one way or the other, stress eventually creeps in. When you learn to be committed, first to God and then to your situation, you'll soon notice a calm in the midst of life's chaos.

"When you are committed and God is invited to be a part of your decision, He will help you meet the challenge."

Be Blessed! Be Inspired!

NOTES

_____

_____

_____

_____

_____

_____

_____

_____

_____

_____

_____

_____

_____

_____

_____

_____

_____

_____

DAY 10

Is It Time to Let Go?

Sometimes it is hard to let things go. For some, forgiveness can happen quickly, offenses left behind and a person moves on. For others, it may be a daily ongoing process, continuing to forgive which means not holding an offense over someone's head and moving on.

A lack of forgiveness can negatively impact your physical and emotional well-being, and can keep you from an intimate relationship with Christ. So, maybe you're saying or thinking what if the other person doesn't deserve forgiveness? God did the forgiving long before you did the repenting. God knew in advance of his act of loving forgiveness that millions and millions of people over the ages would reject His act of love, but Jesus died for them anyway.

If you've struggled with forgiveness, or forgiving someone during this 30-Day Challenge to do THE WORK, talk to God about it and let it go.

"Forgiveness is something you can do even if the other person is unwilling to accept it."

Be Blessed! Be Inspired!

NOTES

_____

_____

_____

_____

_____

_____

_____

_____

_____

_____

_____

_____

_____

_____

_____

DAY 11
It's Attainable

I believe God given goals can make a difference in your life and as you've continued to do THE WORK on your 30-day challenge, you have probably quickly realized this as well. You have taken the first step as you sensed in your heart that something needed to be better or different. You set the goal and have pursed it for 11 days. Truthfully, ideas are cheap everybody has an idea, but turning an idea into a goal is a totally different story.

Success is turning a good idea that God has given you into reality. That requires a goal, and a goal simply is something that you write down; something that you know is doable; and something you know is tangible. You see it, touch it and smell it. It should have an end, a deadline to get there.

Write the vision and make it plane…. "Make it your highest priority to honour God and follow His principles".

Be Blessed! Be Inspired!

NOTES

_____

_____

_____

_____

_____

_____

_____

_____

_____

_____

_____

_____

_____

_____

_____

DAY 12
Hand In Hand

Perhaps doing THE WORK is working on your relationship with your spouse or significant other. When a couple doesn't have a sense of direction in their marriage or relationship a purpose beyond today, it's easy to look for other things to fill that void in their lives. But when you're in agreement, powerful things can happen.

When a couple really sees a long-term vision from God for their lives, they can work together toward the future. Set some goals, 1) Goal, know where the finish line is and agree where you're going; 2) Plan, know what steps you need to take to get from point A to B, and 3) Sacrifice, tradeoffs are necessary in your marriage or relationship if you really want to get there together. Take time today to discover what your spouse needs in order to travel the journey together.

"Walk it out, hand in hand, together"

Be Blessed! Be Inspired!

NOTES

_____

_____

_____

_____

_____

_____

_____

_____

_____

_____

_____

_____

_____

_____

_____

DAY 13

Tapping Into God's Purpose

I really believe God has a wonderful purpose for your life. The key is to be able to tap into it and to put it into motion. So how do you do that? It happens through the decisions you make daily. Where is your focus? What is on your mind? Make your pursuit for God's intentions, intentional. Read your bible and more specifically be obedient to his word.

"A diligent search of scripture can reveal God's intentions for your circumstances"

Be Blessed! Be Inspired!

NOTES

_____

_____

_____

_____

_____

_____

_____

_____

_____

_____

_____

_____

_____

_____

_____

_____

DAY 14
Keep On Keeping On!

Changing a habit or fulfilling a commitment sometimes feels like you're pushing a giant boulder up a steep incline. Refuse to be overcome by disappointment and instead, find your courage by looking forward to the future you desire. What changes are you already experiencing as a result of doing THE WORK? Can you see the difference in your relationships as a result? Look how far you've come, and get a picture, a hope of what that can look like in just 12 more days.

Just a few days ago, you were committed, excited and working to be more intentional in your life. Remember that feeling of moving forward? Don't allow discouragement, defeat and a sense of failure to set in as opposition tries to keep you down. Look at each dip in life as an opportunity to recognize God as your strength.

God has given you all need to rise above the challenges standing between you and doing THE WORK.

"Find your courage by looking forward to future you desire".

Be Blessed! Be Inspired!

NOTES

_____

_____

_____

_____

_____

_____

_____

_____

_____

_____

_____

_____

_____

_____

_____

_____

_____

DAY 15

Demonstrate Your Love for Him

Wow! You're halfway through your commitment to do THE WORK for 30 days. This journey is meant to be directional and purposeful. You get up every morning and make decisions about what you are going to do that day; you choose the direction your life is going to take by those actions.

The direction you take ultimately determines your destination. God created you on purpose and filled you with passion to succeed in becoming who He destined you to be. How you live today set the tone for tomorrow and the day after, and the day after that. Your gift to God is the choices you make and the actions you take. What you think, feel and do each and every day demonstrates your love for God.

"It's only when you choose a direction for your life that pleases Him that you can move from mediocrity to really living the way he intended".

Be Blessed! Be Inspired!

NOTES

_____

_____

_____

_____

_____

_____

_____

_____

_____

_____

_____

_____

_____

_____

_____

_____

DAY 16
Choose to Do the New

We tolerate bad habits because they require no additional effort on our part. As you've discovered by doing THE WORK over these past two weeks, it takes effort to change a habit. I am so excited to know that you are intentionally choosing to replace that bad habit with a good one.

As you press on in your 30-day challenge today, I want to remind you that a bad habit developed over time limits you and limits God's ability to use you. Each day as you do THE WORK continue to choose to do something new.

Do whatever it takes to develop the necessary habits that will create sustain daily action, to live out your purpose.

"Discover your purpose, Glory God and love others".

Be Blessed! Be Inspired!

NOTES

_____
_____
_____
_____
_____
_____
_____
_____
_____
_____
_____
_____
_____
_____
_____

DAY 17

Remember What Made Your Relationship Great

If you're working on something that will benefit your marriage during this 30-day challenge, discontentment is really one of the first serious signs that something bad is about to happen in a marriage relationship (this can be said of other relationships as well). Discontentment In any relationship, friends, co-workers, siblings or parents results when you stop doing what made the relationship successful in the first place. It's vitally important that you don't stop doing the things that you used to do to make your marriage and/or relationship great. Maybe you think, I'm not getting that I think, I should get. This isn't what I bargained for. My expectations have not become reality and I'm discontented.

If you're married, make it a point to go back to the basics and do some of the things that used to do to make your marriage great. If you're struggling in another relationship ask what first drew or connected you to that person and use those things to rebuild on.

"Now godliness with contentment is great gain".

1 Timothy 6:6

Be Blessed! Be Inspired!

NOTES

_____

_____

_____

_____

_____

_____

_____

_____

_____

_____

_____

_____

_____

_____

_____

DAY 18

What You Say and Do Matters

People are trying to find their purpose in life. No matter what your job is, God wants to use you in His ministry and His ministry is people. Whatever God has called you to do, wherever He's placed you to do it, use it to His glory.

Do your actions add to people's lives? Do you offer affirmation, inspiration and hope? Are you equipping them from the overflow of joy in your heart that comes from knowing Christ?

People need to connect with one another and hear the Truth in a loving way. Whether you mean to or not, you share the Good News through your actions. Believers and nonbelievers are watching you. What you say and what you do every day really matters.

"Strive to live intentionally for Christ by being aware that what you say and do really does matter".

Be Blessed! Be Inspired!

NOTES

_____

_____

_____

_____

_____

_____

_____

_____

_____

_____

_____

_____

_____

_____

_____

_____

DAY 19
Strip Off the Weights

In preparation for what's next to come sometimes you have to strip down by removing everything that is weighing you down in order to make it light. Some of those weights include: worry, fear, anxiety, to much work, over commitment, to much entertainment. You can be tempted to load your life with lots of stuff while trying to run the race with a full backpack. It slows you down.

As you continue your 30-day challenge, take a few minutes today and consider if there are some weights in your life that God is prompting you to lay aside. If so, set them down as your press forward to finish the last leg of this 30-day race.

"There is freedom to run your race when you strip off the weights".

Be Blessed! Be Inspired!

NOTES

_____

_____

_____

_____

_____

_____

_____

_____

_____

_____

_____

_____

_____

_____

_____

_____

_____

DAY 20

Use Your Emotions In a Healthy Way

No doubt you've experienced some emotion as you've chosen to do THE WORK these last 20 days. You know how it goes.... Something occurs, a thought or event and you react to it. Your emotions need attention every day. Stress is a negative response everyone has when faced with run-away emotions. It's a physical reaction to life that comes back to our bodies.

Success in life depends on how well you manage your emotions. Your emotions are a result of your thoughts about what is going on around you. Your thoughts lead to your behaviour. When you choose to think and behave like Christ, you can use your emotions to bring God honour.

"Only then can you fuel your emotions to light a fire of passion that will honour God and bring peace to your mind".

Be Blessed! Be Inspired!

NOTES

DAY 21
You and I Are the Why

John, the disciple Jesus loved, says that God's great love for us compelled Him to sacrifice His only Son, which gave us security in knowing we belong to God and our relationship with him is assured (John 3:16-18).

God gave you eternal life. That's his gift to you whether you choose it or not. If you choose to accept His gift, then you should want to give your life back to Him. Intentional Living, doing those things that please him, is your gift back to Him. Your decision to be intentional or not comes down to what you do in response to your love for God.

"Good words and a great speech is not enough. It's taking what you know, caring about others enough to take action and doing something that demonstrates God's love to them".

Be Blessed! Be Inspired!

NOTES

_____

_____

_____

_____

_____

_____

_____

_____

_____

_____

_____

_____

_____

_____

_____

_____

DAY 22

Yes, You Belong

Little children give a vivid picture of an often-unexpressed need inside of us even though our adult lives to belong. Young children unashamedly express this need. They want their parents to give them lots of attention, to watch over progress toward success and to share their lives.

"Mom, look what I made!"

"Daddy, look at me. I can ride a bike with no hands."

That's the way God wired us. As adults, most of us have found it can be a cold, cruel world that greets us when we step outside our homes. As we get older, we have a tendency to express this desire less and less and eventually even as believers, sometimes feel as though we don't have a place where we belong. That's why it's imperative that we find our confidence in our relationship with Christ.

The Bible is full of affirmations that demonstrate that you belong. The Creator of the entire universe loves you. He cares deeply about everything that happens to you in your lifetime. You have a place reserved in God's affections.

"The one who made the oceans, the mountains, the moon and stars loves you!".

Be Blessed! Be Inspired!

NOTES

_____

_____

_____

_____

_____

_____

_____

_____

_____

_____

_____

_____

_____

_____

_____

_____

_____

_____

DAY 23
Praying for You

Have you experienced a lot of interruptions and distractions during your 30-day challenge? Honestly, there are times that the distractions and interruptions are truly beyond your control. As you reflect over the last few weeks, I hope that you were able to say that you, for the most part, were deliberately and proactively in pursuit of doing THE WORK.

I am continually praying for you and support you through this challenge. I continue to ask God to help your take the time to zero and help you focus as you THE WORK. I'm trusting God that doing THE WORK is making a big difference everyday in your relationships that you, as well as your friends and family are seeing God's hand on you.

Please know that doing THE WORK is worthy of the energy you pour into it. You have probably seen changes in your thoughts, feelings and behaviour already. I am thrilled that you have taken Ephesians 5:10, have figured out what pleases Christ, and are doing it today.

"Choose today how you will live before life chooses for you".

Be Blessed! Be Inspired!

NOTES

_____

_____

_____

_____

_____

_____

_____

_____

_____

_____

_____

_____

_____

_____

_____

DAY 24

Generations of Faith

If you are a parent, you hope that your children will always be willing to listen to your counsel. You also know that you won't always be in a position to give it. It's a great comfort to know that God can go with your children where you many not be able to go.

When God becomes your child's personal teacher and mentor, peach is the result. In your dreams of happiness for your children, isn't that really what you want for them?

Life can be tough, even for Christians. God didn't promise to insulate us from the troubles of this world. You can't provide environments for your children that are void of conflict, but you can lead them to an incredible inner source that will sustain them during tough times.

"If you give a child, generations of faith as his background, you give him the ultimate head start in life."

Be Blessed! Be Inspired!

NOTES

_____

_____

_____

_____

_____

_____

_____

_____

_____

_____

_____

_____

_____

_____

_____

DAY 25

THE WORK In Your Faith

In the past three weeks or so, I hope you've been encouraged with the simplicity to focus on doing THE WORK. So many times' when you want to make changes in your life, you are tempted to look at the enormity of the big picture. While It's important to have the big picture for long term, it can sometimes overwhelm you. Looking at doing THE WORK you can do breaks off any discouragement and allows you to see your goal as altogether manageable.

Doing THE WORK can bring results in any area of your life you focus on. As you seek to make Christ the centre of your life, faith is one of the five essential areas of life where you want to be intentionally growing and improving. But when you become overwhelmed with all that you want to change, the enemy often tells you that it's not even worth starting. You are almost there in the 30-day challenge. Don't give up! You can do this!

Don't let that kind of discouragement, that lie get in the way of deepening your faith. As you've discovered throughout this challenge, doing THE WORK in your faith today can lead you into the kind of vibrant, intimate walk with God that you desire.

"Take your faith to the next level by doing THE WORK!". Be Blessed! Be Inspired!

NOTES

_____

_____

_____

_____

_____

_____

_____

_____

_____

_____

_____

_____

_____

_____

_____

_____

DAY 26

Remember God's Compassionate Care

Before you close out this 30-day challenge, I want to talk to you again about forgiveness. When you've been hurt emotionally by a loved one's words, or set back mentally by a lack of trust shown to you, you can feel angry. Even as you've stayed committed to doing THE WORK this month, you may have experienced this. The last thing you want to give that person is grace, unmerited love, or forgiveness, and that's a normal response that comes out of our human nature.

But responding with love is exactly what God asks you to do. Let your memory serve you here and remember the underserved and undying love you've received from Jesus. He responded to you with a compassionate care so strong that He was willing to die for you. The same great God who gave His life for you will help you forgive those closest to you, those same people who can hurt you the most.

Try to see your loved one through God's eyes. Turn your hurt over to God so he can heal and restore you. Consider writing a letter of forgiveness for the person who has hurt you. Read it back to God in prayer and carefully listen as He speaks to you.

"For God so loved the world that he gave his one and only Son, that whoever believes in him shall not perish but have eternal life." John 3:16 Be Blessed! Be Inspired!

NOTES

_____

_____

_____

_____

_____

_____

_____

_____

_____

_____

_____

_____

_____

_____

_____

_____

DAY 27

Daily Decisions Determine Your Destiny

As a believer your decisions are really a continuation of working out your salvation. Your choices about whom you marry, where you live, whether or not to accept Christ as Lord and Saviour all add up to who you are today. The good news is you can change something today and redirect the course of your future.

"You become the product of the decisions you make".

Be Blessed! Be Inspired!

NOTES

_____

_____

_____

_____

_____

_____

_____

_____

_____

_____

_____

_____

_____

_____

_____

DAY 28

Hit the Reset Button

Often as you pursue the intentional life in Christ, it helps to take a step back periodically and think about your actions and decisions. Your commitment to THE WORK over these past four weeks has most likely tested your resolve, patience and stamina.

The philosopher Socrates observed that "the unexamined life is not worth living." A powerful thought, but self-examination is tough and often emotionally unpleasant.

To stay sharp and effective, you must schedule time to reflect and then be prepared to hit the "reset" button. Ask yourself questions about the choices you made and answer honestly in what ways you were most effective with doing THE WORK. In your prayer time ask God to help you carefully examine your heart through your personal evaluation. Make the adjustments he shows you to make and then hit the rest button.

"Give yourself grace and mercy and start again".

Be Blessed! Be Inspired!

NOTES

_____

_____

_____

_____

_____

_____

_____

_____

_____

_____

_____

_____

_____

_____

_____

DAY 29

Prayer Backed by the Power of God

The prophet Elijah was identified in Scripture as a man of God, chiefly because he was first a man of prayer. Imagine how many lives were literally saved through God's answer to Elijah's fervent prayers.

Elijah's prayers had purpose because

He was in regular communication with God.

He prayed for God's will to be accomplished, not his own.

He was persistent, never giving up.

Such prayer, backed by the very power of God, starts with your choice to make prayer a priority, and then following through with that commitment. Choose today to make prayer the foundation of your relationship with God, and the means through which His mighty power and purpose is unleashed.

"When you are determined to make prayer a daily dynamic part of your life, your heart will change, and others will be impacted by your actions."

Be Blessed! Be Inspired!

NOTES

_____

_____

_____

_____

_____

_____

_____

_____

_____

_____

_____

_____

_____

_____

_____

DAY 30
Share Your Hope with Others

CONGRATULATIONS! You successfully completed your 30-day challenge. I hope by doing THE WORK each day, you have seen an amazing difference in your life and the lives of those you love.

We live in a world today that wrestles with what it means to experience hope. As you have grown in Christ during these past 30 days, I pray you were encouraged to share your hope in Christ with other as you did THE WORK each day to become a better you.

The Bible says, without wavering, let us hold tightly to the hope we say we have, for God can be trusted to keep his promise. Think of ways to encourage one another to outbursts of love and good deeds. And let us not neglect our meeting together, as some people do, but encourage and warn each other, especially now that the day of his coming back again is drawing near (Hebrews 10:23-25).

You can give others the exhilarating opportunity to experience hope, freedom, peace, and purpose in Christ like they've never had before. Please share with me and others how your 30-day challenge has impacted you. Your story can inspire others to do THE WORK that can impact their lives, just as I hope this challenge has impacted you!

NOTES

About The Author

Dr. Toi Dennis is a native of Champaign, Illinois, Dr. Dennis' dedication to education and her service to the community has helped her to charter an accomplished and well-rounded career. She is an advocate of social change and a history maker. She believes in displaying the spirit of excellence in everything that she does, and is relentless in her quest to help to positively transform the lives of people and communities. Dr. Dennis is the Founder of Serenity House Women's Shelter Inc. founded December 2012 in Clarksville Tennessee, an educator, author, radio personality, motivational speaker and is one of the most up and coming influential, inspirational and trailblazing leaders of her generation.

Dr. Dennis has over 17 years of experience in Human Services and teaching in Higher Education. She has managed several different programs that were designed to enhance the quality of life for all children and families, and she has conducted research on homelessness and the effects it has on children's mental and behavioural health. As an Educator and Human Service Professional, Dr. Dennis has been most recognized for her passion for establishing relationships in disenfranchised communities, building bridges for underserved populations and serving as an advocate for those whose voices will never be heard.

Dr. Dennis is a 2020 Distinguished Alumni Award Recipient, 2019 Women Who Rock Nashville Nominee, 2018

Community Award Recipient, 2017 Victoria Sutherland Impact Award Recipient, 2017 Not Easily Broken Award Nominee, 2016 Angel Award Finalist Business Woman of The Year Nominee, 2016 Roselyn Jaffe Award Nominee, 2016 NAACP Home Town Hero Recipient, 2015 Governor Volunteer Star Award Recipient, 2013 -2014 Omega Psi Psi Citizen of The Year Recipient, 2014 Leading Lady Honoree and a 2014 SHERO of the month.

For Bookings and Media Inquires, visit www.drtoi.com

Your Inspirational Notes

_____

_____

_____

_____

_____

_____

_____

_____

_____

_____

_____

_____

_____

_____

_____

_____

_____

_____

Your Inspirational Notes

Your Inspirational Notes

_____

_____

_____

_____

_____

_____

_____

_____

_____

_____

_____

_____

_____

_____

_____

_____

_____

Doing The Work To Become A Better You!

Your Inspirational Notes

_____
_____
_____
_____
_____
_____
_____
_____
_____
_____
_____
_____
_____
_____
_____
_____
_____

Your Inspirational Notes

_____
_____
_____
_____
_____
_____
_____
_____
_____
_____
_____
_____
_____
_____
_____

Your Inspirational Notes

_____

_____

_____

_____

_____

_____

_____

_____

_____

_____

_____

_____

_____

_____

_____

_____

_____

_____

_____

Your Inspirational Notes

Doing The Work To Become A Better You!

Your Inspirational Notes

_____

_____

_____

_____

_____

_____

_____

_____

_____

_____

_____

_____

_____

_____

_____

_____

_____

Your Inspirational Notes

_____

_____

_____

_____

_____

_____

_____

_____

_____

_____

_____

_____

_____

_____

_____

_____

Your Inspirational Notes

_____

_____

_____

_____

_____

_____

_____

_____

_____

_____

_____

_____

_____

_____

_____

_____

Your Inspirational Notes

_____

_____

_____

_____

_____

_____

_____

_____

_____

_____

_____

_____

_____

_____

_____

_____

Made in USA - Kendallville, IN
1079167_9798635475959
04.14.2020 0822